I AM. . .
Meditations

We become what we think about

Gracemarie Cirino

Artwork by Donna Hollinshead

Dear Ann Marie,
Finding peace in being~
Love,
Gracemarie

DEDICATION

To all who have inspired me
by being themselves

Jerry Warren,
My loving husband,
I am so grateful for
your encouragement and support,
for making me believe in myself and in
the value of my poetry,
for inspiring me to publish.

Judith Lindquist
Thank you for your reassurance
throughout the process,
for lovingly editing my words
to make my finished product a work of art.

Donna Hollinshead
Much gratitude
for your beautiful artwork and
your guidance throughout
the self-publishing journey.

Gerardine Benedetto
Amy Kathryn Fitzsimmons
Michael Rainone
Fran Doughty
Thank you for your creative ideas and suggestions
that helped shape my work.

Dear Reader,

When I first sat down to meditate in front of the plaque containing the words, I AM…, I asked myself "So who are you today?" That day was the first day that the answer to that question came in the form of a poem. The poem began with "I AM…" and became my intention for the day.

This book contains poems which formed a basis for my daily purpose. In response to what they became for me, I have provided space under each poem for you to fill in your intention for the day.

The poems are not compiled in any particular order so you can open to any page on any day and set your intention from the poem on that page.

Enjoy in peace - and just be.
Gracemarie

I welcome correspondence about my meditative poetry at **gcirino2019@gmail.com**.

.

I AM Whole
One
with every
cell of my body
One
with my breath
One
with my spirit
My mind flits
off like a child
in a meadow
but returns and
sits for a while
before flitting again
But all the time
I am at peace -
at one
I am whole

Today I AM. . .

I AM Compassion
For myself
For others
Our blemishes
Our foibles
We're all in
this together
Family
Friends
Strangers
All have
foibles
All have
strengths
All have
burdens
Look and
finally see
I am compassion

Today I AM. . .

I AM New Year's Day
A new start
Begin again
Fresh from
the oven
Opportunities await
How about a
New Month's Day
or
a New Week's Day
or
a New Day
today
A new start
Begin again
Opportunities await
I am new year's day

Today I AM...

I AM Overwhelmed
Being hit from
all sides
Confusion
Anger
Loss
envelops me
possesses me
Break the cycle
from within
Grow peace
Promote "now"
Explode calm
like a dandelion
Inner overcomes outer
I am overwhelmed

Today I AM. . .

I AM the Dream
Envision it
Think it
Believe it
Aware of it
as it grows within
Then move it
into hands and feet
and movement
in another
now or two
(a few nows from
this now)
It will appear
It will be
The vision
the thought
the belief
materialized
I am the dream

Today I AM. . .

I AM Diverted Stream
But it was comfortable
travelling in
that direction
Not this way!
Stop
Notice the diversion
Relish it
Breathe it
Look around
Observe the
nature of the
distraction
Departure
from the intended path
gives new life
to the journey
Meandering the path
otherwise not taken
It may be a blessing
Don't fight it
I am diverted stream

Today I AM. . .

I AM Reflection
All whom I love
have affected me
All I see
and breathe
and taste
continues to
change me
to become me
I send it all
back out
in all I do
and say
and am
I am reflection

Today I AM. . .

I AM Valuable
Worth beyond measure
Value beyond price
Not in the doing
but
in the be-ing
I am
for me
for others
value-able
for who I am
not for what
I can do
I am valuable

Today I AM. . .

I AM Efficiency
Busy and overwhelmed
collide
All breaks loose
Nothing gets done
Give it
to the universe.
Peace seeps down
All is accomplished
I am efficiency

Today I AM. . .

I AM Mountain Weather
Cold
Warm
Breezy
Still
Changing often
never stagnant
Life is good
Life is difficult
Don't get attached
It will change
Life & change. . .
Synonymous
I am mountain weather

Today I AM. . .

I AM Billions of Moments
A lifetime made up
of seconds
Each of value
in itself
So many got past
without notice
Busy in my mind and
not being in the present
They come and go
never to return
Overlook
or
ignore
and it's gone
Cherish
and it may
remain in memory
I am billions of moments

Today I AM. . .

I AM H$_2$O
Phasing through life
Frozen
to the spot
Rigid, unbending
reacting to
pressure and
bitterness while
attempting to grow
Flowing and Clear
Giving life and
sustenance to those
encountered in my
winding path through life
Totally Free
Filling the space available
Moving with the
heat of passion
for life
All three are the same me
I am H$_2$O

Today I AM. . .

I AM Guitar
Often strummed
Sometimes plucked
or tapped
or pounded
Needing care
and
renewal
at times
to produce
new music
Feel the echo
and
vibration
inward and outward
from plucking and caring
I am guitar

Today I AM. . .

I AM The Day Off
No pretense
No façade
Delicious
Refreshing
Just me
No concern
for acceptance
or approval
Not needing to prove myself
All me
Naked me
Always enough
I am the day off

Today I AM. . .

I AM Branches
Reaching out
while
staying connected
Balancing while
swaying in the wind
Making room to
grow
Adding to the
beauty
of the surroundings
Blossoming & sleeping
in cycles
Greeting the dawn
with open arms
I am branches

Today I AM. . .

I AM Recovery
My amazing body
Sometimes
healing
itself
Sometimes needing help
But often
providing its own
remedy
for trauma
All that is needed
is the patience
to wait
and
to watch
Be in awe
I am recovery

Today I AM. . .

I AM Now
Freed from the past
From regrets
frights
mistakes
Unburdened by the future
By demands
questions
fear
Now is uncomplicated
peace-filled
all there is
Current reality
only reality
to take with me
Minute by minute
Now
I am now

Today I AM...

I AM Release
Let it go
The pain
The anger
Let it flow
out
Exhale
the anxiety
that
eats away at my soul
Accomplishes nothing
Causes dis-ease
within
Let it flow out
Serenity
is restored
I am release

Today I AM. . .

I AM Listening
Everything
everyone
is speaking
To become quiet
enough to
hear my life
in the voices
of the animals
In the sounds
of nature
In the cry
of the poor
In the rumblings
within
Is to live with
an open mind
and heart
I am listening

Today I AM. . .

I AM Flowers in the Forest
If there is
no one to see them
are they beautiful?
If I write a poem
and there is
no one to read it
is it still a poem?
If I have gifts
and do not share them
are they still gifts?
Encouraging the
view of the beholder
is the pain and joy
of beauty
I am flowers in the forest

Today I AM...

I AM Energy
Silence is
needed to
take it in
It leaves me as I
Listen
Talk
Walk
Do
Care
Quiet time
is needed
to recover and
get it back
Be still
and know
Energy returns
I am energy

Today I AM. . .

I AM Yes
Yes to the past
and to the future
Especially
yes to this moment
So simple to
just be
now
Be at one
with the universe
Accept
who I am
where I am
at this moment
No fear
No resistance
No anger
Just yes
and peace
I am yes

Today I AM. . .

I AM Forgiveness
Of myself
Of others
Can I forgive
myself
if others cannot. . .
will not?
Who have I hurt?
Some, I do not know
Can I be sorry for
what I don't
know I did?
Can I forgive others?
Then I can
forgive myself
in their name
I am forgiveness

Today I AM. . .

I AM Still
It is the only
peace I have
I'm not what
is to come
Not
yesterday's
"I should have..."
Here is
where I want to stay
All day
No fears
No regrets
Just here
Nothing upsetting
about this moment
A great "place"
to be
Whenever that is. . .
I am still

Today I AM. . .

I AM Observing
Me
Chatter in
my head
Silence within
and
around me
I see into
now
Noticing
people – animals – plants
Life in all
its wonder
When truly seeing
all worries cease
I am here
and
now
I am observing

Today I AM…

I AM Instrument
How will God
play me today?
How will she use
me to make music?
Who will hear
my music?
I'll rarely know
None of my business
I am simply
producing the melody
that the Musician knows
someone
needs to hear
It may sound off tune
to me
but may
need to be heard
by another
I am instrument

Today I AM. . .

I AM Shields Up
Protect what flows
to and from me
Keep out negativism
hate
unintended reactions
to my actions
Energy flows
from me
Don't let it
become depleted
Renew and refresh it
from the earth
from within
Stay whole
in a world
which can shatter
I am shields up

Today I AM. . .

I AM Off Track
Some bump in the rails
threw me off
Don't know what it was
Can't understand
my feelings
or
my attitude
or
my actions
Nothing seems whole
I am not aligned
Bring soul
and spirit back
What will renew?
How can I re-align?
What is important?
I am off track

Today I AM...

I AM Trust
Trust in life
In process
That there
is a reason
for most everything
Patience that
all is
unfolding as
it should
That I am
where I
need to be
That answers
are over-rated
Questions are
where we live
Trust the questions
I am trust

Today I AM. . .

I AM Waiting
For health to return
For the rain to stop
the birds to chirp
the line to move
the traffic to clear
the sun to rise
But while waiting
I enjoy
the smells
the sounds
the sights
the energy
the silence
the warmth
the peace
now
I am waiting

Today I AM. . .

I AM Many
Kind, compassionate
loving, caring
Yet sometimes
caustic
cutting
unkind
Who is who?
Who wins out?
I relish being one
Dread the
other being seen
Yet. . .
I am many

Today I AM. . .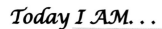

I AM Here
Where I am
may be good
or bad
Light place
or
dark place
No matter
My spirit
guides me
through
as I move from
place to place
bowing before
my spirit
Asking for guidance
from dark to light
from light to dark
I am here

Today I AM. . .

I AM Hands
Open to receiving
and being used
for giving
Needing each other
to complete
most tasks
Reaching out
taking in
and giving
Expressing openness
and
forgiveness
Connecting
with others
with a loving touch
I am hands

Today I AM. . .

I AM Transition
Moving on
Closing a door
Opening another
Endings are
beginnings
Aware of
emotions
No judgments
just awareness
Change is
inevitable
Cling to nothing
Open and close
in gentleness
and peace
Move forward
Smile at what's
behind and
see it for what it is
I am transition

Today I AM. . .

I AM Holy Ground
Walking
Standing
Sitting
Kneeling
Wherever I am
is holy
In this moment
whoever is here
is holy
Sacred
just because
it is
All life
All decision
All change
takes place
on Holy Ground
In Sacred Space
Tread with reverence.
I am holy ground

Today I AM. . .

I AM a Busy Mind
Travelling here
and there without
my soul
Creating panic
and anxiety within
B R E A T H E
Stop the flurry
Be here and
here only
Look at the flowers
or the snow
Plant your feet on
the earth
You are here
not there
I am a busy mind

Today I AM. . .

I AM an Open Door
Each day a new one
Will I open
it wide
and
accept all?
To creak it
little by little
lessens the flow
of life's joy
and challenge
Push it wide open
and
welcome with open arms
whatever
comes through
I am an open door

Today I AM...

I AM a Ripple
All I think
say
do
sends a ripple
out into
the universe
and changes
everything it touches
Know that it
all matters
It all bears
my signature
I am changing things
One thought
One word
One action
at a time
I am a ripple

Today I AM. . .

I AM You
Having empathy
Expressing compassion
To know what
you feel
To walk in
your shoes
To carry your
burden
Loving who
you love
Dreaming your
dreams
Understanding
your heart
Now I comprehend
your essence
I am you

Today I AM. . .

I AM a Foggy Dawn
I can't see the sun yet
but know it's there
Waiting to warm me
and brighten my day
But the mist remains
wetting my skin
blocking my view
I am in a cloud
floating in a fog
Nothing is clear
It, too, shall pass
rise
and dissipate
The sun shall
soon be seen
through
in
and around
the fog.
I am a foggy dawn

Today I AM. . .

I AM Touch
I "feel" inside and out
Stomach working
Heart beating
Breathing
I feel air molecules
Soft surfaces
Loving touches
My cat
The first sense
I am aware of
in the morning
The last at night
I give and receive
through this sense
Be aware today
of the gift
I am touch

Today I AM. . .

I AM Scent
It really does
possess me
I am bathed
in its beauty
It recalls a
memory
whether or not
I am aware
of it
It makes me stop
and enjoy
If I can linger
it may change
my day
I am scent

Today I AM. . .

I AM a Loose Knot
Untie it before
it gets tight
Before it affects
relationships
and quality of life
Open it
free it
release it
Feel the freedom
Ahhhhh!!
Untie them all
one at a time
What a blessing
I am a loose knot

Today I AM. . .

I AM a Lens
Seeing clearly
or
out of focus
Looking at the
big picture
or zooming in
Taking a narrow view
or panoramic
The day
My life
changes
depending on
the view I choose
I am a lens

Today I AM. . .

I AM. . . All Too Much
Overwhelmed
engulfed
inundated
So many details
problems
consequences
Too much to do
Not enough time
Put it all aside
and take a breath
Take a moment
Breathe deeply
Raise them up
and let them fall
one at a time
Do **this** first
Others will come in order
Some may dissolve
without a second glance
(Wouldn't that be nice?)
I am. . . one at a time

Today I AM. . .

I AM Alive
In you
and
in you
and
even in you
If you encountered me
there is a piece of me
within you.
Learn from it
Grow it
then share it
I am not static
or ever gone
I am young and alive
in all I touched
in all I knew
in all I loved
I am here
I am alive

For Jeane

Today I AM. . .

I AM Consciousness
Aware of how my body moves
Of how it feels when it is still
My thoughts as
they come and go
Conscious of the
transition from one
thought to another
One step to
another
One task to
another
Of energy I emit
Energy I
feel for others
Touch – smell – sounds
around me
bombarding me
What a miracle
to be aware
I am consciousness

Today I AM...

I AM Forest
Life all around me
Decay at my feet
Focus on life
full and green
It says "go"
all around me
Orange and
brown at my feet
tell me
that change
is a constant
Sometimes life
is hidden and
belief in life
is all there is
Then there is
new life
starting again
all around and within me
I am forest

Today I AM. . .

I AM Me
Trying my best
Being imperfect
It's what makes
me - Me
I am compassionate
Kind
Loving
Critical
Controlling
Caring
What I think of
me is most important
Think high
Focus on good
Imperfect will
take care of
itself
I am me

Today I AM. . .

I AM Fire
Bright and warm
Giving out
stillness
light
peace
Consumed in
the giving
Needing care
to keep giving
Dangerous
when out of control
Providing so
many good things
to life
when embraced
with care
I am fire

Today I AM. . .

I AM Photographs

Smile!
Capture the now
before it is then
I am all of them
and
none of them
They contain me
and
I contain them
The moments are
all in my head
The picture awakens
the feelings
of the now that was
so different from
this Now
yet still the same
I am photographs

Today I AM. . .

I AM a Foggy Morning
Can't see the sunrise
although I know
it's there
The air is
damp to my skin
but strangely refreshing
Within an hour
the fog lifts
without any
assistance
from me
The sun is high
over the horizon
A new day
A gift
awaits
I am a foggy morning

Today I AM. . .

I AM One More Time
I want you back
To laugh about
something we both
remember differently
To talk about
what we
didn't mention before
To smile at
the mistakes
we made
To express clearly
what was never said
To ask
"Did you know. . .?"
To seek your wisdom
To embrace
To smile
To be
One more time.

For Rosemary

Today I AM. . .

I AM a Winter Landscape
The leaves are gone
I can see the mountains
and
the animals grazing
on the far hillside
Every branch on every
tree is visible
and open
Focus on the openness
winter provides
The chance to lay
bare the dressings
Letting all that was
hidden come into view
I am a winter landscape

Today I AM. . .

I AM Rooted and Rising
As a tree
firmly seated
on the earth
raising my mind
my arms
my being
to the heavens
Experiencing the
sun and the rain
the breeze and the wind
the good weather
and the bad
I stand firm
and high
through all
shaping and growth
I am rooted and rising

Today I AM. . .

I AM the Rest Between Notes
The silences
between the noise
and rush of
my day
I stand still and
suddenly realize
I am here
this is me
This moment of stillness
defines the deepest me
Let the world
swirl around me
Be the center
of the storm
Just for a while
breathe and be
I am the rest between notes

Today I AM. . .

I AM Awakened
Sound stirs me
Now I am here
Where was I?
Oh, yes,
it was a dream
The reality
of a new day
awaits
Another day to explore
the sensations
of this planet
How many more
awakenings?
How much more
can be explored here?
How many more adventures?
Live and enjoy
Rest comes soon enough
I am awakened

Today I AM. . .

I AM Human
Living with other humans
Sharing lives
Sharing traits
What is seen in another
is in me too
What is loathed about another
is in me too
What is loved about another
is in me too
Only degrees of differences
distinguish us
I am human

Today I AM. . .

I AM Pregnant with my Life
My own life is
growing within me
Each facet
waiting to be born
to be recognized
appreciated
loved
I'm not born
all at once
only piece
by piece
Gently aware
of how much
of me
is still unborn
still to come
I am pregnant with my life

Today I AM. . .

I AM What Really Matters
The earth is
turning too fast
I'm losing my
balance
Too many
things to do
Distractions are
all around me
Stumbles abound
Where am I going?
Stop
Look straight ahead
Recover your focus
The view clears
Strength
balance
direction
return
Time to reconnect
with my source
I am what really matters

Today I AM. . .

I AM the Moon
Light to those
who are
in darkness
Turned away
and within
Living in the dark
Reflected light
is still light
Breathe it in
Enjoy it
Soon life will be
lighted again
For now
use your reflected
light to
show the way
I am the moon

Today I AM. . .

I AM Silence
It speaks
sometimes loudly
but always
truthfully
What I hear
in the silence
of my heart
tells me
who I really am
Tells me where to go
Tells me what is
nourishment
and
what is poison
Helps me to
tip-toe
into the unknown
I am silence

Today I AM. . .

I AM Wholeness
Bring them together
mind – body – spirit
Seems that
when one is healthy
other is not
When that one
needs attention
the others falter
Bring them together
See them in your
mind's eye
Meditate all
three in harmony
When one demands
release
gently bring it back
Keep them together
I am wholeness

Today I AM. . .

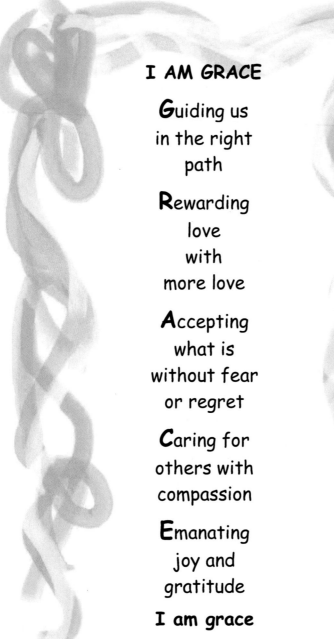

I AM GRACE

Guiding us
in the right
path

Rewarding
love
with
more love

Accepting
what is
without fear
or regret

Caring for
others with
compassion

Emanating
joy and
gratitude

I am grace

For Mommy, from my heart
with love

Made in the
USA
Columbia, SC